BOLD KIDS

Yemen

A VARIETY OF FACTS
CHILDREN'S PEOPLE AND PLACES BOOK

Are you aware of some of the most fascinating Yemen Facts? This book will provide you with a few facts that will make you want to visit this Middle Eastern country. Did you know that Yemen is one of the oldest continuously inhabited cities?

It is an Arab country in Western Asia. Its economy is based primarily on cash. What makes Yemen unique is that it is the oldest continuously inhabited city in the world. And it has the largest cash economy in the world!

YEMEN IS ONE OF THE OLDEST CONTINUOUSLY INHABITED CITIES IN THE WORLD

Sanaa, Yemen is one of the world's oldest continuously populated cities. According to Yemeni legend, Sanaa was first settled by the prophet Shem.

It occupies the site of the ancient preIslamic stronghold Ghumdan, which may date back to the first or second centuries bce. The city subsequently became an important center for Jewish and Christian communities in the Arabian Peninsula, but was later converted to Islam by the fourth caliph ‘Ali’, the son-in-law of the Prophet Muhammad.

IT IS AN ARAB COUNTRY

Yemen is a country in Western Asia and the southern tip of the Arabian Peninsula. It shares borders with Saudi Arabia to the north, Oman to the northeast, and Eritrea, Djibouti, and Somalia on the ocean.

In addition to the Arabian Peninsula, Yemen has two land borders: Oman and Saudi Arabia. Its coastline is almost 3,000 miles long, and it is also the site of the largest humanitarian crisis in the world.

IT IS IN WESTERN ASIA

The climate in Yemen is warm and humid, with little variation from season to season. The temperature can be as high as 37 degrees in some regions and as low as 22 degrees in others. Despite this wide variation, the average temperature is 28 degrees.

The weather in Yemen is relatively pleasant throughout the year, and many people enjoy hiking, diving, and other outdoor activities. Yemen also boasts some of the best diving in the world, including the Red Sea.

IT HAS A LARGELY CASH-BASED ECONOMY

The civil war in Yemen has destroyed the country's critical infrastructure, and its largely cashbased economy has become even more fragile.

Years of mismanagement and corruption have led to chronic poverty and underdevelopment, and more than 70% of Yemenis are now dependent on humanitarian assistance. The war has only worsened the situation, but significant international assistance will likely be needed once the conflict ends. A brief overview of Yemen's economic situation is presented below.

IT HAS NO PRECIPITATION

It's possible to find rain in Yemen despite the fact that this country's climate has been characterized by little to no precipitation.

Yemen's climate is classified by Koppen classification based on native vegetation, temperatures, precipitation, and seasonality. Yemen's rainy season typically falls between July and September but arrived too late in 2021. Flash floods hit Southern Yemen in October, causing havoc and deaths.

IT HAS A POOR ECONOMY

One of the major problems facing Yemen is its poor economy. According to the World Bank, seventy to eighty percent of Yemen's population lives in poverty.

This is comparable to subSaharan Africa and South Asia. But Yemen is much better off than sub-Saharan Africa. Despite the poor economy, Yemen still has an extremely high number of children living in poverty. Fortunately, the government has been working to address these issues.

IT HAS A CIVIL WAR

As the world's attention focuses on the humanitarian catastrophe in the Horn of Africa, few people realize that Yemen has a civil war. Since the start of the conflict in March 2014, foreign forces have been intervening in the country.

The US and Saudi Arabia are reportedly meeting every day to plot the next massacre in the country. Yemen is one of the poorest countries in the region before the Saudis invaded, and now, it's part of the US' war on poverty. But the war rages on largely unnoticed, as the media focuses on the humanitarian crisis and the human costs of war.

CPSIA information can be obtained
at www.ICGtesting.com
Printed in the USA
LVHW051918240323
742527LV00014B/374

9 781071 720738